QUEENDOM
BEAUTIFUL WOMEN (Book #1)

Women are strong, beautiful, intelligent, powerful, and unique. Ten friends get together and rent out a castle for a night of fun, laughter, and friendship. They all share a special crown at the party to celebrate the beauty of being a woman and to embrace the inner beauty of being a queen.

Come listen in on the party. Bring some friends if you like and don't forget your crowns!

Come be inspired and get rejuvenated! Enjoy the adventure, strength, and bond of friendship, sisterly love, and womanhood.

What People Are Saying:

"I really enjoyed the poem "Women Strong". I felt like I could conquer the world after reading this book."

"The poem "Nasty Disposition" had a wonderful twist and a great message. Bravo to the author Precious Won."

"My favorite poem is "Angel Sister", what a powerful poem of friendship and love."

"I felt empowered after reading this book. The poem "Mission Failed" reminded me that I am worthy and to never let anyone put me down. It made me feel good inside and gave me the push I was in need of."

"This is a book you could read over and over again. It's replenishing, uplifting, and refreshing to the soul."

WHAT IS YOUR FAVORITE POEM IN THIS BOOK?

Like on Facebook and talk about your favorite poem @Preciouswonauthor

Visit the author's website at: preciouswontheauthor.com

Also, see (Book #2 and #3) in this series.

QUEENDOM

BEAUTIFUL WOMEN

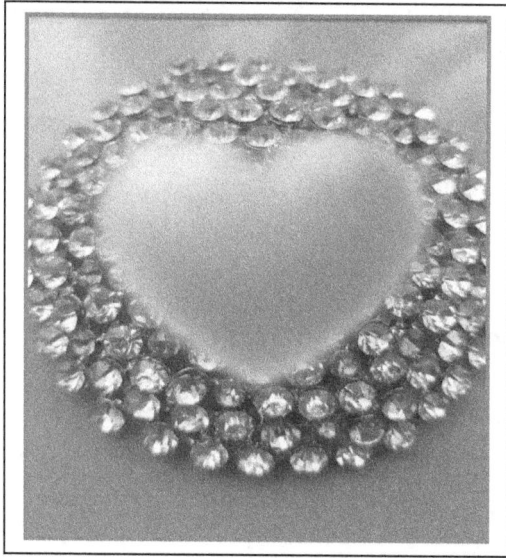

(Women: Strong, Beautiful, Intelligent, Powerful & Unique)

Book #1

By: Precious Won

PALM HANDS PUBLISHING
Corona, California

Published by
PALM HANDS PUBLISHING™
Printed in the United States of America
Queendom Beautiful Women is a trademark of Precious Won.
All rights are reserved.
For information on theater performances, poetry readings,
and speaking engagements visit the website.
Facebook: @Preciouswonauthor
Email: Preciouswontheauthor@gmail.com

Amateur and professional performances of this series (Book
#1, #2, or #3) must be obtained from the author in writing.

This book series is available to colleges and universities at
quantity discounts for bulk purchases.

Library of Congress Control Number: 2018930739
Won, Precious
Queendom Beautiful Women (Book #1)
ISBN-13: 978-0692054727 (paperback)

Visit the website at: preciouswontheauthor.com

DEDICATION

This book is dedicated to young ladies, and women across the world. You are a beautiful queen. Wear your crown well and never let anyone steal your throne. Remember your inner beauty is important and let it shine like the beautiful star you are! Never let anyone belittle you and know that you are precious in so many ways. Just hang in there my queens until your golden day. Stay resilient! If things are tough know that God will always make a way. Remember to help others because that is what queens do, and blessings in return will be bestowed upon you.

CONTENTS

Bonus Journal & A Queen's Anthem

QUEENDOM
BEAUTIFUL WOMEN
(Women: Strong, Beautiful, Intelligent, Powerful & Unique)

Book #1

INTRODUCTION

The lights are dark and as the lights raise up, the scene opens up with ten ladies on stage in a castle. They are all dressed in their beautiful queen garb looking extremely elegant, royal, and powerful. Each woman is poised in a royal stance. *You can hear conga drums, xylophone, and the piccolo playing softly in the background as the ladies begin to speak:*

Queen #1 and #2: We are women strong!

Queen #3 and #4: Beautiful!

Queen #5 and #6: Intelligent!

Queen #7 and #8: Powerful!

Queen #9 and #10: and Unique!

All the Queens: (*Join hands and say in unison.*) These are the things that make us a queen!

All the Queens: (*As they look around the castle*). This sure is a beautiful place!

Queen #1: I thought it would be a great idea if we all got together this year and did something different to celebrate our friendship and the beauty of being a woman. I have a crown that my grandmother passed on to me. She always told me I was a queen. When I was a little girl my grandmother would put the crown on my head and she would share with me all the wonderful stories about great queens all over the world. She told me I was a queen and to never forget it, no matter my circumstances in life. She would always say "search inside for your inner beauty and you will find strength, love, and peace." She said that God gives us inner strength that no one can truly take away, and that there is a queen in every woman.

My grandmother taught me to be resilient because there is good and evil in this world. She said everybody likes easy times, but it's when things get tough, that we must stay strong. She also taught me to give, and not just to receive. My grandmother was so wise and had a beautiful soul. This crown will always remind me of her. I want to share my crown and pass it around to each of you because we are all queens.

Queen #8: Well, I sure feel like a queen wearing this beautiful dress, and that crown is immaculate!

All Queens, except for Queen #1: *All nod in agreement.*

Queen #3: For real girl, these shoes and this dress are off the hook!

Queen #5: Girl and my bling bling, check out this big fancy ring, and all those fancy jewels!

Queen #1: Now ladies you know that a queen is more than shoes, bling, and a pretty dress.

Queen #2: (*Talking to Queen #1*). Take the crown from the table and go to the throne and let us know what a queen is.

All the Queens, except for Queen #1: (*Sing with enthusiasm.*) To the throne you go! To the throne you go! (*They all begin to dance in a circle as music is playing. The music fades and the spotlight is on Queen #1. Conga drums are being played softly as she walks majestically up to the throne. All the other queens are listening intensively as she begins to describe what a queen is.*)

Queen #1

WHAT'S A QUEEN

WHAT'S A QUEEN

A queen is smart
and she has a good heart.
She loves the human race.
She helps the world to
become a better place.

She's more than bling,
rings, and fancy things.
More than designer
purses and fancy shoes,
nails, pedicures,
make-up and hair-dos.
She knows that her
kindness is her
true royal jewel.

She's more than a pretty dress,
always does her best,
never settles for less!

A queen is wise.
She knows that wisdom
not gold or gems
is the valuable prize.

No need to
do provocative things,
be extremely flashy,
or ostentatious to be seen.
She's naturally majestic,
shinning. She is a queen!

The lights raise up and all the other queens begin to clap for Queen #1.

Queen #2: Girl that is so true! A queen is more than a pretty dress, bling, shoes, and purses. In my opinion a queen is defined by her inner beauty.

Queen #1: I think it's time to pass the crown. Come up to the throne and let us know how a queen's beauty is defined. To the throne you go.

All the Queens: (*Sing with enthusiasm.*) To the throne you go! To the throne you go! (*They all begin to dance in a circle as music is playing. The music fades and the spotlight is on Queen #2 as she walks majestically up to the throne. All the other queens are listening intensively as she speaks.*)

Queen #2

HER BEAUTY IS DEFINED

HER BEAUTY IS DEFINED

No need to stick
out her tongue
or show her behind.
Post revealing
pictures of herself online.

Her beauty is defined
because she has a good heart,
an intelligent mind.

She has confidence in herself
and her inner beauty overrides
no need for a million
compliments to feel good inside.

It's in her walk, her talk,
her laugh, her smile
her grace, her hugs,
her love, and her style.
She's strong and fierce,
yet humble all the while.

Her beauty is defined
by her good deeds,
she supports others and
helps those in need.
No time for gossiping or

spreading bad seeds.
Her smile is warm,
and she's well received.

She is precious
because she is kind,
never a phony,
sincere, and divine.

A queen does not
try to impress others.
She's happy and
comfortable being herself.
Her love and good
spirit can always be felt.

She knows it's important
to do and not just say.
Her word is her bond
and defines her
character in so many ways.

No need to second guess her
or read between the lines.
She is clearly magnificent
and her beauty is defined.

The spot light raises up from Queen #2 and we see all the queens in the room. They are all sitting in different positions. They all begin to clap.

Queen #5: Girl I really like that part about not sticking out your tongue. What is that really all about? (*She sticks out her tongue looking silly.*)

All the other Queens: (*Laugh as Queen #5 sticks out her tongue.*)

Queen #3: My favorite part is when she said, "She knows it's important
to do and not just say,
her word is bond
and defines her
character in so many ways."
To me a true queen keeps her word. Some people will tell you, "I got you" or what about, "I will do it tomorrow". Their word is no good.

Queen #7: Music please, (*motioning to Queen #3*). I think it's time for a queen to be heard. Pass the crown and take the throne!

All the Queens: (*Sing with enthusiasm.*) To the throne you go! To the throne you go! (*They all begin to dance in a circle as music is playing. The music fades and the spotlight is on Queen #3 as she walks majestically up to the throne. All the other queens are listening intensively as she speaks.*)

Queen #3
YOUR WORD IS NO GOOD

YOUR WORD IS NO GOOD

Your word is no good,
like a shiny car with no
engine in the hood.
Like a pen that doesn't write
or a bulb that gives no light.

You gave me your word
and said you would,
but you didn't.
Always talking about
"I'm fins to do it right now."
Please, you said that
about a year ago.
You should change your
last name to Unreliable,
nickname Flaky
a.k.a. Undependable.

Said you would help out,
but you're shaky and
questionable without a doubt.

One thing I know is true,
I'm not counting, holding
my breath, or relying on you.

I can't believe or trust
nothing you say.
Your word is like
a river and it
just drifts away.

Like a bad check
denied and unacceptable,
your word is flimsy
and pops like a frigid bubble.

You see a queen's word
is true, dependable,
virtuous, and real,
but that's okay
I love you still.

The spot light raises up from Queen #3 and we see all the queens sitting at the dining table. They all begin to clap.

Queen #4: Girl, I can relate. Don't you hate when people say they're going to do something, but they don't. That's so unqueenly.

Queen #5: I once had a friend who was supposed to pick me up and take me to the airport. She never showed up and I missed my flight. I had a very important job interview.

Queen #7: Well, I once had a guy who said he was picking me up and taking me to this fancy restaurant for my birthday. I took off work early and got all dressed up. I was so excited!!! The sucker didn't even show up or call. He left a queen stranded, but that was okay. I had a plan "B".

All the Queens, except Queen #7: *(Slap hands in unison and laugh.)* A plan "B". I heard that.

Queen #7: Girl, you always have to have a plan "B". Always! Well, I admit I did cry, but just a little bit. Shucks I fell down to the floor crying like a little baby.

I later got back up and had a good time when you ladies came by my house and took me dancing. We were dancing, laughing and I met this really cute guy. I had a real good time that night, thanks to my girls who cheered me up.

Queen #3: Girl you know we were not going to let you sit at home alone on your birthday. All I can say is that your word should be good no matter if you're a man or a woman. A true queen's word is dependable and reliable, like all of you here with me tonight.

All the Queens except Queen #3: Awe!!! Thank you my queen.

Queen #10: Now don't get all sentimental and start making us cry.

Queen #4: Well, get your tissues out because I want to share something with you my queens. (*She looks at Queen #10.*) I was a struggling artist. I loved to paint and draw, but I was not making that much money doing it. You told me to hang in there, the money will come, keep painting and doing what you love. One day I needed art supplies to finish my artwork for a contest.

I was short on money. I didn't want to ask anyone and you just showed up at my door like an angel. You said, "Here take this money and get what you need." I'm not sure how you knew I needed it, but you did. I won first place in the art contest which gave me the exposure I needed. You also supported and helped me by purchasing my art and sharing it on your social media. You were encouraging and didn't give up on me, even when I thought about quitting. You said reach for your inner strength my queen and don't give up. Today I am a successful artist and I have you in part to thank for my success. I want to dedicate this to you.

Queen # 10: Music please. I think it's time for a queen to be heard. Pass the crown and take the throne!

All the Queens except Queen #4: (*Singing with enthusiasm motioning to Queen #4*). Take the crown, to the throne you go! To the throne you go! (*They all begin to dance in a circle as music is playing. The music fades and the spotlight is on Queen #4 as she walks majestically up to the throne. All the other queens are listening intensively as she speaks.*)

Queen #4
ANGEL QUEEN

ANGEL QUEEN

You are truly a queen.
You help people,
no need to be
acknowledged or seen.

You do things
from your heart and
with you love is found.
You put smiles on
people's faces, and help
to erase their frowns.

You help and
give to others
because you are
truly sweet, not
for interior motives
or to receive publicity.

You're an angel queen
and so radiantly you glow.
You're beautiful and
it naturally shows.

Nice and pleasant things
are the words that come
from your mouth.
You encourage others
who are feeling low and
that are in self doubt.

You're beautiful inside and
out, yet you're not conceited.
You interact with people
like the way you
want to be treated.

You're an "Angel Queen"
glistering like a star.
Stay sweet and pleasant
like the queen you truly are.

The spot light raises up from Queen #4 and we see all the queens in the room. They are all sitting in different positions. They all begin to clap.

Queen #10: My queen you know you need to put that on a hallmark card. (*Chuckles after she speaks*).

Queen #4: All of you ladies are supportive, positive, and encouraging. You're the best friends a girl could ever ask for.

Queen #5: Did she say "All" of us are positive and encouraging. Somebody in this group and I'm not saying who, used to have a nasty disposition. They thought they were better than everybody else in this room, and a whole lot of other people. Somebody was bougie. I'm just messing with you (*as she eyes at Queen #6*). I' said used to. You know you have changed for the better my friend. I'm just saying you can't be calling yourself a queen if you have a bad attitude.

All Queens except Queen #5: I think it's time for another queen to go up to the throne. Pass the crown.

All the Queens except Queen #5: (*Sing with enthusiasm.*) To the throne you go! To the throne you go! (*They all begin to dance in a circle as music is playing. The music fades and the spotlight is on Queen #5 as she walks majestically up to the throne. All the other queens are listening intensively as she speaks.*)

Queen #5
NASTY DISPOSITION

NASTY DISPOSITION

You have a nasty disposition,
always having something
smart aleck to say.
A nasty disposition
you need to change
your salty ways.

You have a nasty disposition.
You just need to
shut your mouth.
We all know you gone
say something cynical
without a single doubt.

Always criticizing people
on everything they do.
You need to do some soul
searching and analyze you.

Always looking for
trouble, trying to
start some mess.
You like to
cause confusion and
unnecessary stress.

Ms. Nasty Disposition
this is my advice to you,
help others, be sweet
try being kind.

Stop talking all that
smack and leave
the pettiness behind.

You want people
to help and support
what you do, but you
don't help others, its
always about you.

"Hey everybody look at me,
look what I can do
I'm tooting my own horn
and closing my eyes
and ears to you".

You call yourself
a queen, but the qualities
have yet to been seen.

You see a true queen
is in touch with her
inner soul, heart and mind.
Vanity, rudeness, and
selfishness is not
becoming or divine.

She doesn't need people
to constantly compliment
her on her looks, by
telling her that she's fine.

No need to keep
looking in the mirror,
staring all the time.

With a sprinkle of hope,
and a magic wand, presto
let the negativity disappear.
Let all the goodness and
love come from your
heart, poof let it appear.

Ms. Nasty Disposition,
has transformed to
Ms. Delightful, a
true queen was
always inside.
She learned to put
all the bitterness,
jealousy, back stabbing,
and hatred to the side.

Now that she is pleasant
her true blessings will arrive.

.

The spot light raises up from Queen #5 and we see all the other queens in the room. They are all sitting in different positions. They all begin to clap.

Queen #6: Ok I admit, I used to have a bad attitude and a nasty disposition, but because you were my true friend you set me straight and told me exactly like it was. You didn't sugar coat it. You said girl straight up "You have a nasty disposition, and a funky attitude." You were right my queen (*talking to Queen #5*). I want to thank you for being a true friend and helping me bring out that strong queen who was always inside of me. In fact when my attitude changed, so did my life. I found out when I blessed others, blessings were also bestowed upon me. You have to take time out of your life to help and support others. I have learned not to be selfish and self-centered. Life does work in a 360 and your karma is important. No longer do I relish or celebrate the failures of others. I don't hate nor am I jealous of their success. I am truly happy for people when they succeed, this is all a part of being and developing yourself as a true queen. I'm more mature, wiser and happier. Thank you again my friend (*takes Queen #5 hands.*) for helping me see and understand this. I was the one who did you wrong and I had the nerve to get mad and have an attitude. You didn't just abandon or defriend me. You supported and uplifted me.

Your love, kindness, compassion, and understanding really helped me change for the better. Sometimes you have to take a long honest look at yourself in the mirror. You can't always blame others for your problems or downfalls. I was the one who needed to correct myself. I was going through some unhappy and unpleasant things in my life. I was attacking everyone around me because I was feeling miserable. It took some time for me to realize that when you do a person wrong, apologize and the sooner the better. You must also ask for forgiveness and try to make amends. One of the worse things to do, is to pretend like nothing happened or you were the one who was mistreated. I am truly sorry for the bad things that I said and did to you. I am so grateful that you forgave me and continued to be my friend. Can I please give you a big hug? (*She reaches out to Queen #5 and they hug each other.*)

All the other Queens: (*Smile and clap in joy as Queen #5 and #6 hug each other*).

Queen #5: It's okay we have to learn to forgive and not hold grudges. I admit I was mad. I prayed for you and I forgave you.

Go ahead it's alright my friend lift the heavy burden from your heart. We are all here to listen and help. We're not here to judge you.

Queen #6: Well, I thought I could impress people with name brand items like designer shoes, and purses. Sometimes I over spent to impress others. I thought people would like me more because of the car I drove and the house I lived in. I was trying so hard to impress people with my job, degrees, and materialistic things. I was so stuck-up and full of myself because people were constantly telling me that I was attractive. I tried to pretend that I was happy, but I wasn't. All the material things I bought gave me temporary joy, but I still felt empty and void inside. You told me it is my inner beauty that I should focus more on, and then and only then will I truly be happy. You were so right! I no longer felt the need to impress others. I used to be in constant competition and wanted to always outdo the next person. I was trying to keep up with the Joneses. I had to be better in everything, and this created a stressful state of mind for me. I have now learned to relax and to enjoy being myself. Life is so much better!

I also discovered that some people only wanted to be around me because of my prestige and money. They didn't really like me and were being phony. I know who my true friends are, and they are all right here in this room. The friendship that I have with all of you has meant so much to me over the years. I want to let you all know that you are more than just my friends, you are my sisters.

Queen #1: I think it's time to pass the crown.

All the Queens except Queen #6: (*Sing with enthusiasm.*) To the throne you go! To the throne you go! (*They all begin to dance in a circle as music is playing. The music fades and the spotlight is on Queen #6 as she walks majestically up to the throne. All the other queens are listening intensively as she speaks.*)

Queen #6
YOU ARE MY SISTER

YOU ARE MY SISTER

You are my sister.
You are my friend,
and I won't blow
away like the wind.

I won't disappear
like a thief in the night,
and I'll try my best
to make everything alright.

If you need someone
to chat with don't
hesitate to call.
I don't care what the
hour is, don't think
about it or stall.

Never hesitate if you
need me I'm here.
I want you to understand
this, I want to make it clear.

Do know, I
understand if you
make a mistake.
I won't judge you,
I'm not perfect,
believe me I can relate.

If you need a shoulder
to cry on or someone to
hang out with for fun
just call on me my sister,
you know that I'm the one!

I will help you
whenever I can.
I'll be there to
lift your spirit
when you feel
you can't stand.

I'm your sister and
I got your back.
You can believe this,
one hundred percent fact!

If we argue, get
mad and disagree,
that's okay, you can
still count on me.

You are my sister,
you are my friend.
You can trust me, and
on me you can depend.

I won't gossip your
business that you told
me in confidence.
I'm wiser than that
girl, you know
I have sense.

I love you and
I want you to know,
to me, you
can always go!

I'm here through
thick and thin,
to the very end.
You are my sister,
more than just
my friend.

The spot light raises up from Queen #6 and we see all the queens in the room. They are all sitting in different positions. They all begin to clap.

Queen #6: I also want to sing a song and dedicate it to all of you. It's called, "You are my sister, my friend". *(Queen #6 begins to sing to all the other queens. When she finishes they all come together and hug.)*

Queen #7: Awe! Girl that's what friends are for to help and support each other in good and bad times.

Queen #2: You know we are your girls and what we say is only out of love, never spite. We truly care about you and your happiness. Some friends are fair weather friends, and very judgmental, but we've got your back! As women we must learn to love and help our fellow sisters as we journey through life.

Queen #7: I am so glad you ladies are not fair weather friends. Remember that time I was having a hard time meeting Mr. Right. You ladies told me to slow down and put a lock on it. I was mad at first telling each and every one of you to stay out of my business and to stay in your own lanes. Deep down inside I knew you all just wanted the best for me and was giving me some good advice out of love. Well, I have learned to act more queenly and to slow down. I have learned to have more discretion and to stop running around giving my queenly goods away to every man I meet. I am saving my love.

Queen #1: I think it's time to pass the crown.

All the Queens except Queen #7: (*Sing with enthusiasm.*) To the throne you go! To the throne you go! (*They all begin to dance in a circle as music is playing. The music fades and the spotlight is on Queen #7 as she walks majestically up to the throne. All the other queens are listening intensively as she speaks.*)

Queen #7
SAVING HER LOVE

SAVING HER LOVE

She is keeping her
legs closed tight.
She's saving her love
until she meets Mr. Right.

She's keeping her
legs closed and you can't
see what's in between,
this queen is saving her love
for a mighty strong king.
One who will treat her with
respect, she'll be his everything!

She's not giving her
heart to a little boy,
who wants to play
with her like a toy.
She's giving her heart
to a real man who
wants to bring her joy.

She's saving her love
for the one, that is
faithful and will stay,
not a joker who clowns,
plays games then runs away.

This queen is
saving her love.
A king will
come my way
and together will
ride out to the sunset
to cherish our special day!

The spot light raises up from Queen #7 and we see all the queens in the room. They are all sitting in different positions. They all begin to clap.

Queen #8: Nobody is perfect (*talking to Queen #7*). You got yourself together. Look at you now! We all go through love changes. Don't give up on love! Not all men are bad, and some will treat you really good. They are kings. They are handsome, true, protective, loving, and kind. You keep saving your love for the right one. You will meet your king someday. I'm glad you redeemed yourself. Just because you made a mistake in life, doesn't mean you have to keep messing up and doing the same wrong things. I am a true testimony of that. I have made some mistakes in my life. I'm not perfect. Sometimes people sacrifice their morals and who they truly are in exchange for materialistic things, emotional desires, and money. I want to share something entitled "Redeem Your Crown".

Queen #1: I think it's time to pass the crown.

All the Queens except Queen #8: (*Sing with enthusiasm.*) To the throne you go! To the throne you go! (*They all begin to dance in a circle as music is playing. The music fades and the spotlight is on Queen #8 as she walks majestically up to the throne. All the other queens are listening intensively as she speaks.*)

Queen #8
REDEEM YOUR CROWN

REDEEM YOUR CROWN

What happened to the old you?
The you who believed in something,
the you that had dreams and a purpose.

The you who was strong,
who believed in life,
family, culture, and God.

You sold your soul.
The "It" and the Vultures
took you over and
now they control you.

You do and say
things that are,
really not you.

But I know you. Your spirit
can be awaken, and the
spell can be broken!
I'm praying for the old you
to come back and
redeem your crown.

The spot light raises up from Queen #8 and we see all the queens in the room. They are all sitting in different positions. They all begin to clap.

Queen #9: Yes, Lord we all make mistakes, but it's good to know that if we truly want to make a change and with the power of prayer we can get back to being that queen that we truly are. Sometimes we drop our crowns, but we can pick that crown right back up like the strong queens that we are!

Queen #10: That's right, pick that crown right back up!

Queen #9: However, sometimes people will try to push you down and make you feel like less. They want to steal your crown, happiness, and peace. I don't stand for that.

Queen #1: Nobody is going to push you around (*talking to Queen #9*). I know your spirit, and your will is very strong. I think it's time to pass the crown.

Queen #9: You know it! Don't even try to break me down!

All the Queens: (*Sing with enthusiasm.*) To the throne you go! To the throne you go! (*They all begin to dance in a circle as music is playing. The music fades and the spotlight is on Queen #9 as she walks majestically up to the throne. All the other queens are listening intensively as she speaks.*)

Queen #9

MISSION FAILED

MISSION FAILED

Did you think I would be shaky
like a fish out of water,
trembling in my skin?
Well think again my friend.

Did you think I would
be scared to death,
eyes big like Buckwheat?
Sorry but you missed that treat.

You thought I would
be crying like a baby,
miserable and bent over?
Well you keep wishing
on that four leaf clover.

I'm strong and I don't
believe in doing wrong
because in the end I know
victory will be my song.

The power of God is in me
and I can't be torn down,
this makes you angry
resentful and you frown.

You keep shooting arrows
at me and missing,
all the time wishing
you can get me to act a fool,
hoping I'll lose my cool

but it's not working,
so you keep searching
for other tools.

Constantly trying to stab me
in my heart with your
nasty and untruthful words,
but I keep singing happily
like a morning bird.

You stole from me,
fired me, and tried to
tarnish my name
but I kept my head up high
strong all the same.

You said you would teach
me a lesson, because I
didn't bow down to you
and that you would make
my life painful, miserable, and blue.

You thought I would retaliate,
but I know violence is not the way.
Success is the best revenge
and so I'm going about my day.

I'm smiling at peace
and you don't understand why.
You thought your dirty
ways would make me
roll over and die.

You wanted me to
feel tiny and small,
well my Lord makes
me feel ten feet tall.

You keep trying
to push me down, and
put me in my place,
break my spirit,
and take my joy away.
But I keep getting right back up,
and you're not having any luck.

You might as well give in,
call it quits, throw in the towel,
and raise the white flag,
because quitting is something
I don't put in my bag.

Let me go ahead and
break this down to you,
it's becoming quite apparent
that you don't have a clue.

I don't stop until victory is won.
"I Never Give Up", is my favorite song.
Yes I'm worthy. I have my
crown. I earned my throne,
and I will forever, forever... march on!

You thought you could
make me feel like less,
well jokes on you
because I'm totally blessed,
and your trifling vindictive ways
I don't even stress.

You thought I would be begging,
I guess you'll stay craving.
You can't buy me,
because my soul is not for sale,
and in the end your attempts
to destroy me, will be "Mission Failed".

The spot light raises up from Queen #9 and we see all the queens in the room. They are all sitting in different positions. They all begin to clap.

Queen #10: Mission Failed. I like that. You go girl! My queen! You know we women have to stick together and support one another. Some people want us to feel powerless and weak, but we must stay strong as we make our journey through life. I want to dedicate this to all of you beautiful queens here tonight and all the women across the world.

Queen #1: It's time to pass the crown.

All the Queens: (*Sing with enthusiasm.*) To the throne you go! To the throne you go! (*They all begin to dance in a circle as music is playing. The music fades and the spotlight is on Queen #10 as she walks majestically up to the throne. All the other queens are listening intensively as she speaks.*)

Queen #10
WOMEN STRONG

<u>WOMEN STRONG</u>

Women, Strong, Beautiful, Intelligent, Powerful
and Unique, these are the words that describe
me.

Don't call me
out my name,
a bitch, or a hoe,
respect me, or
you have to go!
I'm a queen,
thought I'll let
you know.

I have my own mind,
and yes I can think.
I can make my own
money, so don't
try to belittle me.

Women are strong, beautiful, intelligent,
powerful and unique, these are the words that
describe queens.

We give birth
and help to
replenish this world.

Women are the ones
who give life to
boys and to girls.

Life that we
nurture, that comes
from our bodies our flesh.
Women are unique and
should always be cherished.

Making sacrifices, helping
others, going the extra mile!
Exhausted, yet still able to smile.

We work hard, be it as
a mother, wife or in a career,
some of us do it all with
endurance, might, and fierce!

Loving, encouraging, caring
hanging in there
and giving it our all.
We do our best to
keep everything together,
this is just one of our calls.

We own businesses, run organizations,
scientist, engineers, politicians,
stay at home moms, lawyers, teachers, athletes,
entertainers, doctors, astronauts, CEO'S, we can
do it all!

Women let's stand tall,
pick each other
up my sister if we get
discouraged, tired or fall.

We are bold when
we need to be, yet
also nice and sweet.
Supporting one another
in sisterhood with
love and unity!

We won't roll over
because were not weak
and we won't satisfy
your faulty ego by
pretending to be meek.

We have a voice, opinions
and we shall speak!
No, I will not allow you
to bully and intimidate me.

Together we stand
strong hand in hand.
No disrespect, or hatred
do know that we love our men.

Women, Strong, Beautiful, Intelligent, Powerful
and Unique, these are the things that make us a
queen!

The spot light raises up from Queen #10 and we see all the queens in the room. They are all sitting in different positions. They all begin to clap.

As they are clapping, a king comes on stage and bows down to Queen #7. The trumpets are playing and fades out softly. He unrolls a scroll and begins to read from it.

King: Rise my queens
and go faithfully
after your dreams.
Don't get discouraged
no matter how hard it seems.
With faith, hard work, and prayer
you will conquer your goals.
Happiness, peace, and love
is yours as declared
on this scroll.

Queen #7: I think my king has arrived.

All other Queens: I thought you were slowing down and saving your love.

Queen #7: I said I was saving my love for a king. He has come my way and I'm about to ride off to the sunset, so excuse me ladies. Look, Snow White got kissed by a prince and they rode off happily ever after on the same day they met. How come I can't have my king and ride off to the sunset on the same day? I have a gut feeling that this king will respect, love, protect, and cherish me. It's not like you meet a king every day.

King: My queen I will respect, love, protect, and cherish you. You see, if it were not for a woman, I would not be here. A man did not carry me in his womb. My mother carried me for nine long months. She nourished, kept me safe, and allowed me to be born into this world. Every king needs a queen, and for some reason out of all the women here in this castle I walked up to you. It must be faith. Will you, beautiful lady be my queen?

All the other Queens: Girl I'll say.

Queen #5: Sounds like a bunch of tired lines.

Queen #7: (*Looks back at her friends, then turns to the king and says*) Look here's my number. Let's get to know each other better before we ride off to the sunset. Let's do coffee or lunch and get more acquainted. I have to get back with my queens. We can talk later.

King: No rush my lovely queen (*as he bows down to her and kisses her hand*). You are obviously worth waiting for and getting to know better. By the way, a little bird told me that you like yellow roses. I will make sure to bring you a dozen of beautiful yellow roses when we meet again my queen. (*The king exists the stage.*)

Queen #7: (*Blushes and smiles*).

Queen #5: (*Talking to Queen #7*). Girls those tired lines. I'm just being silly. I hope you find true love, just be careful and don't move to fast. Take your time my queen.

Queen #7: I most definitely will take my time and get to know him better. I also, want him to get to know me. He does have a wonderful smile and he is so charming. My King Charming!

King: *(Runs back on stage).* Did someone call my name? I heard somebody say King Charming. *(Bows and says)* I am at your service.

Queen #5: *(Brushes the king off stage with a hand movement and says)* No. Not yet King. Not yet. She said she wants to get to know you better.

Queen #7: I can speak for myself. You have my number. We can talk later Mr. King Charming.

King: *(The king smiles and kisses Queen #7 hand as he exits the stage.)*

Queen #1: Ladies I think we need to get some sleep because we have to get up early and check out. This castle is not cheap. However, before we go to sleep, I want you all to know that you are my friends, my queens and I mean it from the bottom of my heart. I want women all over the world to know that you too are queens. Life is not perfect, and nobody is perfect, but one thing is for sure, never let anybody steal your inner beauty. Know that you are a queen, and happiness as well as peace is yours to have.

No matter your current situation in life, know there is a queen inside of you. Get to know her, love her, cherish her and never let anyone devalue her! (*All the other Queens begin to stand up and clap loudly! The applause fades and Queen #1 continues to speak.*)
Proclaim her and protect her. It doesn't matter if you are in a castle or in the slums. If you are rich or if you are poor. No matter the shade of your skin, you are beautiful and there is a queen within you!

One more thing my queens before we depart, I have nine gifts to bestow upon you ladies. These gifts hold many different aspects of life, but have patience do not open them yet. We will all open them together when we meet again.

Queen #4: Why wait let's open the gifts now.

Queen #5: Yeah, let's open them now!

Queen #6: Can we just take a peek? I wonder what's inside.

Queen #9: Can you at least give us a hint? The suspense is killing me.

Queen #1: No, you must wait. Patience is a virtue. Now come on ladies let our voices be heard.

All the queens step up together they begin to dance and sing the song "Queens All Over The World". At the end of the song each woman is poised in a royal stance. (You can hear conga drums, xylophone, and the piccolo playing softly in the background as the ladies begin to speak.)

Queen #1 and #2: We are women strong!

Queen #3 and #4: Beautiful!

Queen #5 and #6: Intelligent!

Queen #7 and #8: Powerful!

Queen #9 and #10: and Unique!

All the Queens: *(Join hands and say in unison.)* These are the things that make us a queen! Women all over the world you are queens!

Lights fade down and the Queens exit on royal music.

ACKNOWLEDGEMENTS

Inspirational Credits:
God
My Mom
My Grandmothers
Women all over the world

**ROYAL
ANNOUNCEMENT**

QUEENDOM
BEAUTIFUL WOMEN

The Royal Purple–Good & Evil

Book #2

Get Book #2 and find out what the nine gifts were that Queen #1 gave to the other queens. Also, there are a lot of surprises, secrets, excitement, and adventures!

About The Author

Precious has received several accolades for her poetry including the prestigious Jessie Redmon Fauset Book Award. She is a motivational speaker and is known for her famous inspirational poems "Mission Failed", "Who Really Won the Prize", "Don't Give Up" and "I'm Right Here". Her poem "I Made My Peace With God" is a favorite of many of her readers. Precious's poetry is relatable, understandable, inspirational, powerful, and compassionate. Her writing style and ability to connect with her readers and audiences has many referring to her as "The People's Poet". Additionally, her poetry has been featured on greeting card scrolls in Hallmark Stores.

The author also toured with a performing arts group. Her favorite role was Queen Cleopatra. Besides her first love for writing, she has a very diverse background in the arts which includes acting, dancing, and singing. Her acting, singing, and dancing roots began at Marla Gibb's CrossRoads Arts Academy and Theater in Los Angeles. At a very early age Precious was exposed to the arts by her parents and she was mentored by Angela Gibbs who recognized her writing abilities and acting skills as a young teenager.

She is a trained vocalist and studied dance under several instructors including Karen McDonald. She does dance choreography and is also a freelance songwriter. She also has a fashion background and was a model and buyer for Real Deal Clothing and Jewelry line.

Additionally, Precious is a graduate of the University of Southern California (USC) and truly has a strong love and passion for music. When she is not writing, she enjoys family time, the beach, football, having lunch with friends, listening and playing the piano and teaching acting and vocal classes.

This author does the majority of her writing during spring which is her favorite time of the year and adores her garden that includes beautiful arrays of flowers which she personally planted and cares for. Her flowers that bloom so elegantly during the spring, the beautiful weather and of course her favorite coffee accounts for her burst of writing during the spring season.

Precious is also a strong advocate of education and encourages literacy. You can visit her website at: preciouswontheauthor.com

---

A QUEEN'S INNER BEAUTY IS HER TRUE TREASURE

My Favorite Poems

"QUEENDOM BEAUTIFUL WOMEN"
Get Book #1 #2 and #3

My Favorite Two Poems

"Queendom Beautiful Women Book #1"

1._____
2._____

"Queendom Beautiful Women Book #2"

1._____
2._____

"Queendom Beautiful Women Book #3"

1._____
2._____

Go online where you purchased the book and leave a review of your favorite two poems. Visit the website at: Preciouswontheauthor.com

****

Get an Autograph Copy of this book:

Author's Autograph: _____
Bring your books to one of my events for an opportunity to get my autograph.

Other Books By the Author Precious Won:

Emotion SuperMarket A Series of Poetry (Book #1)

Emotion SuperMarket A Series of Poetry (Book #2)

Emotion SuperMarket A Series of Poetry (Book #3)

Sunshine, Flowers & The In Between - Book #1
  (Inspiration and Hope)

Sunshine, Flowers & The In Between - Book #2
(Love and Second Chances)

Sunshine, Flowers & The In Between - Book #3
(Peace and Happiness)

*Queendom Beautiful Women (Book #1)

Queendom Beautiful Women (Book #2)

Queendom Beautiful Women (Book #3)

"A Queen's Inner Beauty Is Her True Treasure"

MY QUEEN JOURNAL
(BONUS JOURNAL)

I have included a bonus journal in this book so that you may reflect on your inner beauty and the things that truly make you a queen. Additionally, I have included "A Queen's Anthem" for women to appreciate, get in touch with, and love themselves internally. Your inner beauty can provide strength, love, and peace, because in every woman there is a queen!

Outer Beauty vs. Inner Beauty

There is nothing wrong with taking care of your outer beauty. If you decide to wear your hair curly, in an afro, straight, in braids, long, or short that is your choice. If you want to wear make-up or if you prefer not to wear any at all that too is your choice. You can be light, dark, or medium in skin complexion, but your outer skin color does not define your character. You can have a lot of money or hardly none, and that will not define you as a person.

Materialistic things, and how you look on the outside does not define you or your happiness. It is your inner beauty that truly defines you. Beauty is as beauty does, it is not based on how good you look in the mirror.

Also, to be a queen you must first learn to love yourself. Don't always be in need of others to validate or reassure you. A queen knows who she is and doesn't constantly need people to tell her that she is beautiful to feel good about herself or to determine her self worth. While it is important to love yourself, you must also love and help others. A true queen is never selfish or self-centered.

No matter where you were born or where you live, be it in a mansion, in a small apartment, uptown, or downtown, know that what makes you a queen is your inner beauty not your location.

Being fashionable or focusing on your outer appearance may be important to you, but make sure you focus just as hard, if not harder on your inner beauty. Your outside beauty will fade, but your inner beauty will live on.

In closing self-love and valuing yourself is important. Remember, it is not your looks, money, or where you live, but it is your good deeds, and inner beauty which truly makes you a queen. Wear your crown well and walk up to the throne!

A QUEEN'S THRONE

A QUEEN'S ANTHEM

What's a queen? A queen is smart and she has a good heart. She is more than a pretty dress, always does her best, and never settles for less! She is not defined by money or materialistic things, and is more concerned about giving than being seen. ***Her beauty is defined*** no need to second guess her character or read between the lines. You will never tell her ***"Your word is no good"*** because she knows it's important to do and not just say. Her word is her bond and defines her character in so many ways. She is an ***Angel Queen***, and with her true love is found. She put smiles on people's faces, and helps to erase their frowns. A ***nasty disposition*** in a true queen you will never find, she is in touch with her inner beauty, heart, soul, and mind. She knows that vanity, and rudeness is not becoming or divine.

"You are my sister" is what she tells her friends and she will love and support you to the very end. She reflects on the proverb "As a ring of gold in a swine's snout, so is a lovely woman who lacks discretion", therefore she's doesn't act loose, wild, or reckless. She seeks to do good and never wrong. She is **_saving her love_** for the right person to come along. A king that is faithful and will stay, not a joker who clowns, plays games then runs away. **_Redeem your crown_** is what she tells herself if she makes a mistake, as she moves toward self-improvement, while helping others along the way. She has confidence and knows her self worth. She is a queen regardless of where she was born or lives on this earth. Never try and make a queen feel like less, because it will be **_mission failed_**, as she is totally blessed. **_Women strong_** is something she understands. She wishes love and peace to all her sisters across the lands. She knows that her inner beauty is her true jewel, but don't take her kindness for weakness, because she's nobody's fool. She is strong, beautiful, intelligent, powerful and unique, and these are the things that make her a queen!

MY QUEEN JOURNAL

(I am a queen)

"No one can steal the inner beauty and strength I have inside. No matter my current situation, with God I will survive."

_____

_____

_____

_____

_____

_____

_____

_____

_____

_____

_____

_____

_____

_____

_____

_____

_____

MY QUEEN JOURNAL

(I am a queen)

"No one can steal the inner beauty and strength I have inside. No matter my current situation, with God I will survive."

_____

_____

_____

_____

_____

_____

_____

_____

_____

_____

_____

_____

_____

_____

_____

_____

_____

_____

_____

_____

MY QUEEN JOURNAL

(I am a queen)

"No one can steal the inner beauty and strength I have inside. No matter my current situation, with God I will survive

_____

_____

_____

_____

_____

_____

_____

_____

_____

_____

_____

_____

_____

_____

_____

_____

_____

_____

_____

_____

_____

MY QUEEN
JOURNAL

(I am a queen)

"No one can steal the inner beauty and strength I have inside. No matter my current situation, with God I will survive."

_____

_____

_____

_____

_____

_____

_____

_____

_____

_____

_____

_____

_____

_____

_____

_____

_____

_____

_____

_____

_____

MY QUEEN JOURNAL

(I am a queen)

"No one can steal the inner beauty and strength I have inside. No matter my current situation, with God I will survive."

_____

_____

_____

_____

_____

_____

_____

_____

_____

_____

_____

_____

_____

_____

_____

_____

_____

_____

_____

_____

_____

_____

_____

_____

MY QUEEN JOURNAL

(I am a queen)

"No one can steal the inner beauty and strength I have inside. No matter my current situation, with God I will survive."

_____

_____

_____

_____

_____

_____

_____

_____

_____

_____

_____

_____

_____

_____

_____

_____

_____

_____

_____

_____

MY QUEEN JOURNAL

(I am a queen)

"No one can steal the inner beauty and strength I have inside. No matter my current situation, with God I will survive."

_____

_____

_____

_____

_____

_____

_____

_____

_____

_____

_____

_____

_____

_____

_____

_____

_____

_____

MY QUEEN JOURNAL

(I am a queen)

"No one can steal the inner beauty and strength I have inside. No matter my current situation, with God I will survive."

_____

_____

_____

_____

_____

_____

_____

_____

_____

_____

_____

_____

_____

_____

_____

_____

_____

_____

_____

_____

MY QUEEN
JOURNAL
(I am a queen)

"No one can steal the inner beauty and strength I have inside. No matter my current situation, with God I will survive."

_____

_____

_____

_____

_____

_____

_____

_____

_____

_____

_____

_____

_____

_____

_____

_____

_____

MY QUEEN JOURNAL

(I am a queen)

"No one can steal the inner beauty and strength I have inside. No matter my current situation, with God I will survive."

_____

_____

_____

_____

_____

_____

_____

_____

_____

_____

_____

_____

_____

_____

_____

_____

_____

_____

_____

_____

MY QUEEN JOURNAL

(I am a queen)

"No one can steal the inner beauty and strength I have inside. No matter my current situation, with God I will survive."

_____

_____

_____

_____

_____

_____

_____

_____

_____

_____

_____

_____

_____

_____

_____

_____

_____

_____

_____

_____

MY QUEEN JOURNAL

(I am a queen)

"No one can steal the inner beauty and strength I have inside. No matter my current situation, with God I will survive."

_____

_____

_____

_____

_____

_____

_____

_____

_____

_____

_____

_____

_____

_____

_____

_____

_____

_____

_____

_____

MY QUEEN
JOURNAL
(I am a queen)

"No one can steal the inner beauty and strength I have inside. No matter my current situation, with God I will survive."

_____

_____

_____

_____

_____

_____

_____

_____

_____

_____

_____

_____

_____

_____

_____

_____

_____

_____

_____

_____

MY QUEEN JOURNAL

(I am a queen)

"No one can steal the inner beauty and strength I have inside. No matter my current situation, with God I will survive."

_____

_____

_____

_____

_____

_____

_____

_____

_____

_____

_____

_____

_____

_____

_____

_____

_____

_____

_____

_____

_____

_____

MY QUEEN
JOURNAL

(I am a queen)

"No one can steal the inner beauty and strength I have inside. No matter my current situation, with God I will survive."

_____

_____

_____

_____

_____

_____

_____

_____

_____

_____

_____

_____

_____

_____

_____

_____

_____

_____

_____

_____

_____

MY QUEEN JOURNAL

(I am a queen)

"No one can steal the inner beauty and strength I have inside. No matter my current situation, with God I will survive."

_____

_____

_____

_____

_____

_____

_____

_____

_____

_____

_____

_____

_____

_____

_____

_____

_____

_____

_____

MY QUEEN JOURNAL

(I am a queen)

"No one can steal the inner beauty and strength I have inside. No matter my current situation, with God I will survive."

_____

_____

_____

_____

_____

_____

_____

_____

_____

_____

_____

_____

_____

_____

_____

_____

_____

_____

_____

_____

_____

_____

MY QUEEN
JOURNAL

(I am a queen)

"No one can steal the inner beauty and strength I have inside. No matter my current situation, with God I will survive."

_____

_____

_____

_____

_____

_____

_____

_____

_____

_____

_____

_____

_____

_____

_____

_____

_____

_____

_____

_____

_____

_____

CPSIA information can be obtained
at www.ICGtesting.com
Printed in the USA
LVHW081308050419
613115LV00018B/244/P

9 780692 054727